Controlled Substance Drug Record

LTC/Rehab/ALFs/CBRFs

ISBN: 9781702819800

Controlled Substance Log

Page #	Resident	Medication	Dose	RX#	Date Received	Nurse	Date Complete
1							
2							
3							
4							
5							
6							
7							
8							
9							
10							
11							
12							
13							
14							
15							
16							
17							
18							
19							
20							
21							
22							
23							
24							
25							
26							
27							
28							
29							
30							
31							
32							
33							
34							
35							
36							
37							
38							
39							
40							
41							
42							

43							
44							
45							
46							
47							
48							
49							
50							

Individual Resident Record

Resident Controlled Substance Record

Resident			Date Received	MD	
Medication		Dose	RX#	Nurse receiving	
Directions for medication			Amount received	2nd Nurse signature	

#	Date	Time	Amount Given	Nurse Signature	Amount Remaining
1					
2					
3					
4					
5					
6					
7					
8					
9					
10					
11					
12					
13					
14					
15					
16					
17					
18					
19					
20					
21					
22					
23					
24					
25					
26					
27					
28					
29					
30					

Medication Disposition Record

Date: _________________ Quantity Destroyed: ___________ Quantity sent with resident: ___________

Nurse 1: ____

Nurse 2: ____

Comments:____

Resident Controlled Substance Record

Resident				Date Received	MD
Medication			Dose	RX#	Nurse receiving
Directions for medication				Amount received	2nd Nurse signature

#	Date	Time	Amount Given	Nurse Signature	Amount Remaining
1					
2					
3					
4					
5					
6					
7					
8					
9					
10					
11					
12					
13					
14					
15					
16					
17					
18					
19					
20					
21					
22					
23					
24					
25					
26					
27					
28					
29					
30					

Medication Disposition Record

Date: _______________ Quantity Destroyed: __________ Quantity sent with resident: __________

Nurse 1: ____

Nurse 2: ____

Comments: ____

<h1 style="text-align:center">Resident Controlled Substance Record</h1>

Resident			Date Received	MD
Medication		Dose	RX#	Nurse receiving
Directions for medication			Amount received	2nd Nurse signature

#	Date	Time	Amount Given	Nurse Signature	Amount Remaining
1					
2					
3					
4					
5					
6					
7					
8					
9					
10					
11					
12					
13					
14					
15					
16					
17					
18					
19					
20					
21					
22					
23					
24					
25					
26					
27					
28					
29					
30					

Medication Disposition Record

Date: _________________ Quantity Destroyed: ___________ Quantity sent with resident: __________

Nurse 1: ____

Nurse 2: ____

Comments: ____

Resident Controlled Substance Record

Resident			Date Received	MD

Medication		Dose	RX#	Nurse receiving

Directions for medication			Amount received	2nd Nurse signature

#	Date	Time	Amount Given	Nurse Signature	Amount Remaining
1					
2					
3					
4					
5					
6					
7					
8					
9					
10					
11					
12					
13					
14					
15					
16					
17					
18					
19					
20					
21					
22					
23					
24					
25					
26					
27					
28					
29					
30					

Medication Disposition Record

Date: ________________ Quantity Destroyed: __________ Quantity sent with resident: __________

Nurse 1: ____

Nurse 2: ____

Comments: ____

Resident Controlled Substance Record

Resident			Date Received	MD	
Medication		Dose	RX#	Nurse receiving	
Directions for medication			Amount received	2nd Nurse signature	

#	Date	Time	Amount Given	Nurse Signature	Amount Remaining
1					
2					
3					
4					
5					
6					
7					
8					
9					
10					
11					
12					
13					
14					
15					
16					
17					
18					
19					
20					
21					
22					
23					
24					
25					
26					
27					
28					
29					
30					

Medication Disposition Record

Date: _________________ Quantity Destroyed: ___________ Quantity sent with resident: __________

Nurse 1: ____

Nurse 2: ____

Comments: ____

<h1 style="text-align:center">Resident Controlled Substance Record</h1>

Resident		Date Received	MD
Medication	Dose	RX#	Nurse receiving
Directions for medication		Amount received	2nd Nurse signature

#	Date	Time	Amount Given	Nurse Signature	Amount Remaining
1					
2					
3					
4					
5					
6					
7					
8					
9					
10					
11					
12					
13					
14					
15					
16					
17					
18					
19					
20					
21					
22					
23					
24					
25					
26					
27					
28					
29					
30					

Medication Disposition Record

Date: _________________ Quantity Destroyed: __________ Quantity sent with resident: __________

Nurse 1: ____

Nurse 2: ____

Comments: ____

Resident Controlled Substance Record

Resident				Date Received	MD	
Medication			Dose	RX#	Nurse receiving	
Directions for medication				Amount received	2nd Nurse signature	

#	Date	Time	Amount Given	Nurse Signature	Amount Remaining
1					
2					
3					
4					
5					
6					
7					
8					
9					
10					
11					
12					
13					
14					
15					
16					
17					
18					
19					
20					
21					
22					
23					
24					
25					
26					
27					
28					
29					
30					

Medication Disposition Record

Date: _________________ Quantity Destroyed: ___________ Quantity sent with resident: ___________

Nurse 1: ____

Nurse 2: ____

Comments: ____

Resident Controlled Substance Record

Resident			Date Received	MD	
Medication		Dose	RX#	Nurse receiving	
Directions for medication			Amount received	2nd Nurse signature	

#	Date	Time	Amount Given	Nurse Signature	Amount Remaining
1					
2					
3					
4					
5					
6					
7					
8					
9					
10					
11					
12					
13					
14					
15					
16					
17					
18					
19					
20					
21					
22					
23					
24					
25					
26					
27					
28					
29					
30					

Medication Disposition Record

Date: _________________ Quantity Destroyed: __________ Quantity sent with resident: __________

Nurse 1: ____

Nurse 2: ____

Comments: ____

Resident Controlled Substance Record

Resident			Date Received	MD
Medication		Dose	RX#	Nurse receiving
Directions for medication			Amount received	2nd Nurse signature

#	Date	Time	Amount Given	Nurse Signature	Amount Remaining
1					
2					
3					
4					
5					
6					
7					
8					
9					
10					
11					
12					
13					
14					
15					
16					
17					
18					
19					
20					
21					
22					
23					
24					
25					
26					
27					
28					
29					
30					

Medication Disposition Record

Date: _________________ Quantity Destroyed: ___________ Quantity sent with resident: __________

Nurse 1: ____

Nurse 2: ____

Comments: ____

Resident Controlled Substance Record

Resident				Date Received	MD	
Medication			Dose	RX#	Nurse receiving	
Directions for medication				Amount received	2nd Nurse signature	

#	Date	Time	Amount Given	Nurse Signature	Amount Remaining
1					
2					
3					
4					
5					
6					
7					
8					
9					
10					
11					
12					
13					
14					
15					
16					
17					
18					
19					
20					
21					
22					
23					
24					
25					
26					
27					
28					
29					
30					

Medication Disposition Record

Date: _________________ Quantity Destroyed: ___________ Quantity sent with resident: ___________

Nurse 1: ____

Nurse 2: ____

Comments: ____

Resident Controlled Substance Record

Resident			Date Received	MD	
Medication		Dose	RX#	Nurse receiving	
Directions for medication			Amount received	2nd Nurse signature	

#	Date	Time	Amount Given	Nurse Signature	Amount Remaining
1					
2					
3					
4					
5					
6					
7					
8					
9					
10					
11					
12					
13					
14					
15					
16					
17					
18					
19					
20					
21					
22					
23					
24					
25					
26					
27					
28					
29					
30					

Medication Disposition Record

Date: _________________ Quantity Destroyed: ___________ Quantity sent with resident: __________

Nurse 1: ____

Nurse 2: ____

Comments: ____

Resident Controlled Substance Record

Resident			Date Received	MD	
Medication		Dose	RX#	Nurse receiving	
Directions for medication			Amount received	2nd Nurse signature	

#	Date	Time	Amount Given	Nurse Signature	Amount Remaining
1					
2					
3					
4					
5					
6					
7					
8					
9					
10					
11					
12					
13					
14					
15					
16					
17					
18					
19					
20					
21					
22					
23					
24					
25					
26					
27					
28					
29					
30					

Medication Disposition Record

Date: _________________ Quantity Destroyed: ___________ Quantity sent with resident: ___________

Nurse 1: ____

Nurse 2: ____

Comments: ____

Resident Controlled Substance Record

Resident			Date Received	MD	
Medication		Dose	RX#	Nurse receiving	
Directions for medication			Amount received	2nd Nurse signature	

#	Date	Time	Amount Given	Nurse Signature	Amount Remaining
1					
2					
3					
4					
5					
6					
7					
8					
9					
10					
11					
12					
13					
14					
15					
16					
17					
18					
19					
20					
21					
22					
23					
24					
25					
26					
27					
28					
29					
30					

Medication Disposition Record

Date: _________________ Quantity Destroyed: ___________ Quantity sent with resident: ___________

Nurse 1: ____

Nurse 2: ____

Comments: ____

Resident Controlled Substance Record

Resident			Date Received	MD	
Medication		Dose	RX#	Nurse receiving	
Directions for medication			Amount received	2nd Nurse signature	

#	Date	Time	Amount Given	Nurse Signature	Amount Remaining
1					
2					
3					
4					
5					
6					
7					
8					
9					
10					
11					
12					
13					
14					
15					
16					
17					
18					
19					
20					
21					
22					
23					
24					
25					
26					
27					
28					
29					
30					

Medication Disposition Record

Date: _________________ Quantity Destroyed: ___________ Quantity sent with resident: ___________

Nurse 1: ____

Nurse 2: ____

Comments: ____

<h2 align="center">Resident Controlled Substance Record</h2>

Resident			Date Received	MD
Medication		Dose	RX#	Nurse receiving
Directions for medication			Amount received	2nd Nurse signature

#	Date	Time	Amount Given	Nurse Signature	Amount Remaining
1					
2					
3					
4					
5					
6					
7					
8					
9					
10					
11					
12					
13					
14					
15					
16					
17					
18					
19					
20					
21					
22					
23					
24					
25					
26					
27					
28					
29					
30					

Medication Disposition Record

Date: _________________ Quantity Destroyed: __________ Quantity sent with resident: __________

Nurse 1: ____

Nurse 2: ____

Comments: ____

Resident Controlled Substance Record

Resident			Date Received	MD

Medication	Dose	RX#	Nurse receiving

Directions for medication	Amount received	2nd Nurse signature

#	Date	Time	Amount Given	Nurse Signature	Amount Remaining
1					
2					
3					
4					
5					
6					
7					
8					
9					
10					
11					
12					
13					
14					
15					
16					
17					
18					
19					
20					
21					
22					
23					
24					
25					
26					
27					
28					
29					
30					

Medication Disposition Record

Date: _______________ Quantity Destroyed: __________ Quantity sent with resident: __________

Nurse 1: ____

Nurse 2: ____

Comments: ____

Resident Controlled Substance Record

Resident			Date Received	MD
Medication		Dose	RX#	Nurse receiving
Directions for medication			Amount received	2nd Nurse signature

#	Date	Time	Amount Given	Nurse Signature	Amount Remaining
1					
2					
3					
4					
5					
6					
7					
8					
9					
10					
11					
12					
13					
14					
15					
16					
17					
18					
19					
20					
21					
22					
23					
24					
25					
26					
27					
28					
29					
30					

Medication Disposition Record

Date: _________________ Quantity Destroyed: ___________ Quantity sent with resident: ___________

Nurse 1: ____

Nurse 2: ____

Comments: ____

Resident Controlled Substance Record

Resident				Date Received	MD	
Medication			Dose	RX#	Nurse receiving	
Directions for medication				Amount received	2nd Nurse signature	

#	Date	Time	Amount Given	Nurse Signature	Amount Remaining
1					
2					
3					
4					
5					
6					
7					
8					
9					
10					
11					
12					
13					
14					
15					
16					
17					
18					
19					
20					
21					
22					
23					
24					
25					
26					
27					
28					
29					
30					

Medication Disposition Record

Date: _________________ Quantity Destroyed: ___________ Quantity sent with resident: ___________

Nurse 1: ____

Nurse 2: ____

Comments: ____

Resident Controlled Substance Record

Resident		Date Received	MD
Medication	Dose	RX#	Nurse receiving
Directions for medication		Amount received	2nd Nurse signature

#	Date	Time	Amount Given	Nurse Signature	Amount Remaining
1					
2					
3					
4					
5					
6					
7					
8					
9					
10					
11					
12					
13					
14					
15					
16					
17					
18					
19					
20					
21					
22					
23					
24					
25					
26					
27					
28					
29					
30					

Medication Disposition Record

Date: _________________ Quantity Destroyed: ___________ Quantity sent with resident: ___________

Nurse 1: ____

Nurse 2: ____

Comments: ____

Resident Controlled Substance Record

Resident				Date Received	MD
Medication			Dose	RX#	Nurse receiving
Directions for medication				Amount received	2nd Nurse signature

#	Date	Time	Amount Given	Nurse Signature	Amount Remaining
1					
2					
3					
4					
5					
6					
7					
8					
9					
10					
11					
12					
13					
14					
15					
16					
17					
18					
19					
20					
21					
22					
23					
24					
25					
26					
27					
28					
29					
30					

Medication Disposition Record

Date: ________________ Quantity Destroyed: __________ Quantity sent with resident: __________

Nurse 1: ____

Nurse 2: ____

Comments: ____

Resident Controlled Substance Record

Resident			Date Received	MD	
Medication		Dose	RX#	Nurse receiving	
Directions for medication			Amount received	2nd Nurse signature	

#	Date	Time	Amount Given	Nurse Signature	Amount Remaining
1					
2					
3					
4					
5					
6					
7					
8					
9					
10					
11					
12					
13					
14					
15					
16					
17					
18					
19					
20					
21					
22					
23					
24					
25					
26					
27					
28					
29					
30					

Medication Disposition Record

Date: _______________ Quantity Destroyed: __________ Quantity sent with resident: __________

Nurse 1: ____

Nurse 2: ____

Comments: ____

Resident Controlled Substance Record

Resident			Date Received	MD	
Medication		Dose	RX#	Nurse receiving	
Directions for medication			Amount received	2nd Nurse signature	

#	Date	Time	Amount Given	Nurse Signature	Amount Remaining
1					
2					
3					
4					
5					
6					
7					
8					
9					
10					
11					
12					
13					
14					
15					
16					
17					
18					
19					
20					
21					
22					
23					
24					
25					
26					
27					
28					
29					
30					

Medication Disposition Record

Date: _________________ Quantity Destroyed: ___________ Quantity sent with resident: ___________

Nurse 1: ____

Nurse 2: ____

Comments: ____

Resident Controlled Substance Record

Resident			Date Received	MD	
Medication		Dose	RX#	Nurse receiving	
Directions for medication			Amount received	2nd Nurse signature	

#	Date	Time	Amount Given	Nurse Signature	Amount Remaining
1					
2					
3					
4					
5					
6					
7					
8					
9					
10					
11					
12					
13					
14					
15					
16					
17					
18					
19					
20					
21					
22					
23					
24					
25					
26					
27					
28					
29					
30					

Medication Disposition Record

Date: ________________ Quantity Destroyed: __________ Quantity sent with resident: __________

Nurse 1: ____

Nurse 2: ____

Comments: ____

Resident Controlled Substance Record

Resident			Date Received	MD
Medication		Dose	RX#	Nurse receiving
Directions for medication			Amount received	2nd Nurse signature

#	Date	Time	Amount Given	Nurse Signature	Amount Remaining
1					
2					
3					
4					
5					
6					
7					
8					
9					
10					
11					
12					
13					
14					
15					
16					
17					
18					
19					
20					
21					
22					
23					
24					
25					
26					
27					
28					
29					
30					

Medication Disposition Record

Date: ___________________ Quantity Destroyed: ___________ Quantity sent with resident: ___________

Nurse 1: ____

Nurse 2: ____

Comments: ____

Resident Controlled Substance Record

Resident			25	Date Received	MD	
Medication			Dose	RX#	Nurse receiving	
Directions for medication				Amount received	2nd Nurse signature	

#	Date	Time	Amount Given	Nurse Signature	Amount Remaining
1					
2					
3					
4					
5					
6					
7					
8					
9					
10					
11					
12					
13					
14					
15					
16					
17					
18					
19					
20					
21					
22					
23					
24					
25					
26					
27					
28					
29					
30					

Medication Disposition Record

Date: _______________ Quantity Destroyed: __________ Quantity sent with resident: __________

Nurse 1: ____

Nurse 2: ____

Comments: ____

Resident Controlled Substance Record

Resident				Date Received	MD	
Medication			Dose	RX#	Nurse receiving	
Directions for medication				Amount received	2nd Nurse signature	

#	Date	Time	Amount Given	Nurse Signature	Amount Remaining
1					
2					
3					
4					
5					
6					
7					
8					
9					
10					
11					
12					
13					
14					
15					
16					
17					
18					
19					
20					
21					
22					
23					
24					
25					
26					
27					
28					
29					
30					

Medication Disposition Record

Date: _________________ Quantity Destroyed: __________ Quantity sent with resident: __________

Nurse 1: ____

Nurse 2: ____

Comments: ____

Resident Controlled Substance Record

Resident			Date Received	MD	
Medication		Dose	RX#	Nurse receiving	
Directions for medication			Amount received	2nd Nurse signature	

#	Date	Time	Amount Given	Nurse Signature	Amount Remaining
1					
2					
3					
4					
5					
6					
7					
8					
9					
10					
11					
12					
13					
14					
15					
16					
17					
18					
19					
20					
21					
22					
23					
24					
25					
26					
27					
28					
29					
30					

Medication Disposition Record

Date: _________________ Quantity Destroyed: ___________ Quantity sent with resident: __________

Nurse 1: ____

Nurse 2: ____

Comments: ____

Resident Controlled Substance Record

Resident			Date Received	MD	
Medication		Dose	RX#	Nurse receiving	
Directions for medication			Amount received	2nd Nurse signature	

#	Date	Time	Amount Given	Nurse Signature	Amount Remaining
1					
2					
3					
4					
5					
6					
7					
8					
9					
10					
11					
12					
13					
14					
15					
16					
17					
18					
19					
20					
21					
22					
23					
24					
25					
26					
27					
28					
29					
30					

Medication Disposition Record

Date: _________________ Quantity Destroyed: ___________ Quantity sent with resident: __________

Nurse 1: ____

Nurse 2: ____

Comments: ____

Resident Controlled Substance Record

Resident		Date Received	MD
Medication	Dose	RX#	Nurse receiving
Directions for medication		Amount received	2nd Nurse signature

#	Date	Time	Amount Given	Nurse Signature	Amount Remaining
1					
2					
3					
4					
5					
6					
7					
8					
9					
10					
11					
12					
13					
14					
15					
16					
17					
18					
19					
20					
21					
22					
23					
24					
25					
26					
27					
28					
29					
30					

Medication Disposition Record

Date: _______________ Quantity Destroyed: __________ Quantity sent with resident: __________

Nurse 1: ____

Nurse 2: ____

Comments: ____

Resident Controlled Substance Record

Resident			Date Received	MD
Medication		Dose	RX#	Nurse receiving
Directions for medication			Amount received	2nd Nurse signature

#	Date	Time	Amount Given	Nurse Signature	Amount Remaining
1					
2					
3					
4					
5					
6					
7					
8					
9					
10					
11					
12					
13					
14					
15					
16					
17					
18					
19					
20					
21					
22					
23					
24					
25					
26					
27					
28					
29					
30					

Medication Disposition Record

Date: _________________ Quantity Destroyed: ___________ Quantity sent with resident: ___________

Nurse 1: ____

Nurse 2: ____

Comments: ____

Resident Controlled Substance Record

Resident			Date Received	MD	
Medication		Dose	RX#	Nurse receiving	
Directions for medication			Amount received	2nd Nurse signature	

#	Date	Time	Amount Given	Nurse Signature	Amount Remaining
1					
2					
3					
4					
5					
6					
7					
8					
9					
10					
11					
12					
13					
14					
15					
16					
17					
18					
19					
20					
21					
22					
23					
24					
25					
26					
27					
28					
29					
30					

Medication Disposition Record

Date: _________________ Quantity Destroyed: ___________ Quantity sent with resident: ___________

Nurse 1: ____

Nurse 2: ____

Comments: ____

Resident Controlled Substance Record

Resident			Date Received	MD	
Medication		Dose	RX#	Nurse receiving	
Directions for medication			Amount received	2nd Nurse signature	

#	Date	Time	Amount Given	Nurse Signature	Amount Remaining
1					
2					
3					
4					
5					
6					
7					
8					
9					
10					
11					
12					
13					
14					
15					
16					
17					
18					
19					
20					
21					
22					
23					
24					
25					
26					
27					
28					
29					
30					

Medication Disposition Record

Date: _________________ Quantity Destroyed: ___________ Quantity sent with resident: ___________

Nurse 1: ____

Nurse 2: ____

Comments: ____

Resident Controlled Substance Record

Resident			Date Received	MD
Medication		Dose	RX#	Nurse receiving
Directions for medication			Amount received	2nd Nurse signature

#	Date	Time	Amount Given	Nurse Signature	Amount Remaining
1					
2					
3					
4					
5					
6					
7					
8					
9					
10					
11					
12					
13					
14					
15					
16					
17					
18					
19					
20					
21					
22					
23					
24					
25					
26					
27					
28					
29					
30					

Medication Disposition Record

Date: _________________ Quantity Destroyed: ___________ Quantity sent with resident: ___________

Nurse 1: ____

Nurse 2: ____

Comments: ____

Resident Controlled Substance Record

Resident			Date Received	MD	
Medication		Dose	RX#	Nurse receiving	
Directions for medication			Amount received	2nd Nurse signature	

#	Date	Time	Amount Given	Nurse Signature	Amount Remaining
1					
2					
3					
4					
5					
6					
7					
8					
9					
10					
11					
12					
13					
14					
15					
16					
17					
18					
19					
20					
21					
22					
23					
24					
25					
26					
27					
28					
29					
30					

Medication Disposition Record

Date: _________________ Quantity Destroyed: ___________ Quantity sent with resident: __________

Nurse 1: ____

Nurse 2: ____

Comments: ____

Resident Controlled Substance Record

Resident			Date Received	MD	
Medication		Dose	RX#	Nurse receiving	
Directions for medication			Amount received	2nd Nurse signature	

#	Date	Time	Amount Given	Nurse Signature	Amount Remaining
1					
2					
3					
4					
5					
6					
7					
8					
9					
10					
11					
12					
13					
14					
15					
16					
17					
18					
19					
20					
21					
22					
23					
24					
25					
26					
27					
28					
29					
30					

Medication Disposition Record

Date: _________________ Quantity Destroyed: __________ Quantity sent with resident: __________

Nurse 1: ____

Nurse 2: ____

Comments: ____

Resident Controlled Substance Record

Resident			Date Received	MD	
Medication		Dose	RX#	Nurse receiving	
Directions for medication			Amount received	2nd Nurse signature	

#	Date	Time	Amount Given	Nurse Signature	Amount Remaining
1					
2					
3					
4					
5					
6					
7					
8					
9					
10					
11					
12					
13					
14					
15					
16					
17					
18					
19					
20					
21					
22					
23					
24					
25					
26					
27					
28					
29					
30					

Medication Disposition Record

Date: _________________ Quantity Destroyed: __________ Quantity sent with resident: __________

Nurse 1: ____

Nurse 2: ____

Comments: ____

Resident Controlled Substance Record

Resident			Date Received	MD	
Medication		Dose	RX#	Nurse receiving	
Directions for medication			Amount received	2nd Nurse signature	

#	Date	Time	Amount Given	Nurse Signature	Amount Remaining
1					
2					
3					
4					
5					
6					
7					
8					
9					
10					
11					
12					
13					
14					
15					
16					
17					
18					
19					
20					
21					
22					
23					
24					
25					
26					
27					
28					
29					
30					

Medication Disposition Record

Date: _________________ Quantity Destroyed: ___________ Quantity sent with resident: ___________

Nurse 1: ____

Nurse 2: ____

Comments: ____

Resident Controlled Substance Record

Resident			Date Received	MD	
Medication		Dose	RX#	Nurse receiving	
Directions for medication			Amount received	2nd Nurse signature	

#	Date	Time	Amount Given	Nurse Signature	Amount Remaining
1					
2					
3					
4					
5					
6					
7					
8					
9					
10					
11					
12					
13					
14					
15					
16					
17					
18					
19					
20					
21					
22					
23					
24					
25					
26					
27					
28					
29					
30					

Medication Disposition Record

Date: _________________ Quantity Destroyed: ___________ Quantity sent with resident: ___________

Nurse 1: ____

Nurse 2: ____

Comments: ____

Resident Controlled Substance Record

Resident		Date Received	MD
Medication	Dose	RX#	Nurse receiving
Directions for medication		Amount received	2nd Nurse signature

#	Date	Time	Amount Given	Nurse Signature	Amount Remaining
1					
2					
3					
4					
5					
6					
7					
8					
9					
10					
11					
12					
13					
14					
15					
16					
17					
18					
19					
20					
21					
22					
23					
24					
25					
26					
27					
28					
29					
30					

Medication Disposition Record

Date: _________________ Quantity Destroyed: __________ Quantity sent with resident: __________

Nurse 1: ____

Nurse 2: ____

Comments: ____

Resident Controlled Substance Record

Resident				Date Received	MD	
Medication			Dose	RX#	Nurse receiving	
Directions for medication				Amount received	2nd Nurse signature	

#	Date	Time	Amount Given	Nurse Signature	Amount Remaining
1					
2					
3					
4					
5					
6					
7					
8					
9					
10					
11					
12					
13					
14					
15					
16					
17					
18					
19					
20					
21					
22					
23					
24					
25					
26					
27					
28					
29					
30					

Medication Disposition Record

Date: _________________ Quantity Destroyed: ___________ Quantity sent with resident: ___________

Nurse 1: ____

Nurse 2: ____

Comments: ____

<h1 style="text-align:center">Resident Controlled Substance Record</h1>

Resident		Date Received	MD
Medication	Dose	RX#	Nurse receiving
Directions for medication		Amount received	2nd Nurse signature

#	Date	Time	Amount Given	Nurse Signature	Amount Remaining
1					
2					
3					
4					
5					
6					
7					
8					
9					
10					
11					
12					
13					
14					
15					
16					
17					
18					
19					
20					
21					
22					
23					
24					
25					
26					
27					
28					
29					
30					

Medication Disposition Record

Date: _________________ Quantity Destroyed: ___________ Quantity sent with resident: ___________

Nurse 1: ____

Nurse 2: ____

Comments: ____

Resident Controlled Substance Record

Resident			Date Received	MD	
Medication		Dose	RX#	Nurse receiving	
Directions for medication			Amount received	2nd Nurse signature	

#	Date	Time	Amount Given	Nurse Signature	Amount Remaining
1					
2					
3					
4					
5					
6					
7					
8					
9					
10					
11					
12					
13					
14					
15					
16					
17					
18					
19					
20					
21					
22					
23					
24					
25					
26					
27					
28					
29					
30					

Medication Disposition Record

Date: _________________ Quantity Destroyed: ___________ Quantity sent with resident: ___________

Nurse 1: ____

Nurse 2: ____

Comments: ____

Resident Controlled Substance Record

Resident		Date Received	MD
Medication	Dose	RX#	Nurse receiving
Directions for medication		Amount received	2nd Nurse signature

#	Date	Time	Amount Given	Nurse Signature	Amount Remaining
1					
2					
3					
4					
5					
6					
7					
8					
9					
10					
11					
12					
13					
14					
15					
16					
17					
18					
19					
20					
21					
22					
23					
24					
25					
26					
27					
28					
29					
30					

Medication Disposition Record

Date: _________________ Quantity Destroyed: ___________ Quantity sent with resident: ___________

Nurse 1: ____

Nurse 2: ____

Comments: ____

<h2 style="text-align:center">Resident Controlled Substance Record</h2>

Resident			Date Received	MD	
Medication		Dose	RX#	Nurse receiving	
Directions for medication			Amount received	2nd Nurse signature	

#	Date	Time	Amount Given	Nurse Signature	Amount Remaining
1					
2					
3					
4					
5					
6					
7					
8					
9					
10					
11					
12					
13					
14					
15					
16					
17					
18					
19					
20					
21					
22					
23					
24					
25					
26					
27					
28					
29					
30					

Medication Disposition Record

Date: _________________ Quantity Destroyed: ___________ Quantity sent with resident: ___________

Nurse 1: ____

Nurse 2: ____

Comments: ____

Resident Controlled Substance Record

Resident		Date Received	MD
Medication	Dose	RX#	Nurse receiving
Directions for medication		Amount received	2nd Nurse signature

#	Date	Time	Amount Given	Nurse Signature	Amount Remaining
1					
2					
3					
4					
5					
6					
7					
8					
9					
10					
11					
12					
13					
14					
15					
16					
17					
18					
19					
20					
21					
22					
23					
24					
25					
26					
27					
28					
29					
30					

Medication Disposition Record

Date: _________________ Quantity Destroyed: ___________ Quantity sent with resident: __________

Nurse 1: ____

Nurse 2: ____

Comments: ____

Resident Controlled Substance Record

Resident			Date Received	MD	
Medication		Dose	RX#	Nurse receiving	
Directions for medication			Amount received	2nd Nurse signature	

#	Date	Time	Amount Given	Nurse Signature	Amount Remaining
1					
2					
3					
4					
5					
6					
7					
8					
9					
10					
11					
12					
13					
14					
15					
16					
17					
18					
19					
20					
21					
22					
23					
24					
25					
26					
27					
28					
29					
30					

Medication Disposition Record

Date: _________________ Quantity Destroyed: ___________ Quantity sent with resident: ___________

Nurse 1: ____

Nurse 2: ____

Comments: ____

<h2 align="center">Resident Controlled Substance Record</h2>

Resident				Date Received	MD	
Medication			Dose	RX#	Nurse receiving	
Directions for medication				Amount received	2nd Nurse signature	

#	Date	Time	Amount Given	Nurse Signature	Amount Remaining
1					
2					
3					
4					
5					
6					
7					
8					
9					
10					
11					
12					
13					
14					
15					
16					
17					
18					
19					
20					
21					
22					
23					
24					
25					
26					
27					
28					
29					
30					

Medication Disposition Record

Date: _______________ Quantity Destroyed: ___________ Quantity sent with resident: ___________

Nurse 1: ____

Nurse 2: ____

Comments: ____

Resident Controlled Substance Record

Resident		Date Received	MD
Medication	Dose	RX#	Nurse receiving
Directions for medication		Amount received	2nd Nurse signature

#	Date	Time	Amount Given	Nurse Signature	Amount Remaining
1					
2					
3					
4					
5					
6					
7					
8					
9					
10					
11					
12					
13					
14					
15					
16					
17					
18					
19					
20					
21					
22					
23					
24					
25					
26					
27					
28					
29					
30					

Medication Disposition Record

Date: _________________ Quantity Destroyed: ___________ Quantity sent with resident: ___________

Nurse 1: ____

Nurse 2: ____

Comments: ____

Resident Controlled Substance Record

Resident			Date Received	MD	
Medication		Dose	RX#	Nurse receiving	
Directions for medication			Amount received	2nd Nurse signature	

#	Date	Time	Amount Given	Nurse Signature	Amount Remaining
1					
2					
3					
4					
5					
6					
7					
8					
9					
10					
11					
12					
13					
14					
15					
16					
17					
18					
19					
20					
21					
22					
23					
24					
25					
26					
27					
28					
29					
30					

Medication Disposition Record

Date: _________________ Quantity Destroyed: ___________ Quantity sent with resident: ___________

Nurse 1: ____

Nurse 2: ____

Comments: ____

Resident Controlled Substance Record

Resident			Date Received	MD	
Medication		Dose	RX#	Nurse receiving	
Directions for medication			Amount received	2nd Nurse signature	

#	Date	Time	Amount Given	Nurse Signature	Amount Remaining
1					
2					
3					
4					
5					
6					
7					
8					
9					
10					
11					
12					
13					
14					
15					
16					
17					
18					
19					
20					
21					
22					
23					
24					
25					
26					
27					
28					
29					
30					

Medication Disposition Record

Date: _________________ Quantity Destroyed: ___________ Quantity sent with resident: ___________

Nurse 1: ____

Nurse 2: ____

Comments: ____

Shift

to

Shift

Count

Nurse to Nurse Controlled Substance Count Verification

Date	Time	Off Going Nurse	On Coming Nurse
Date	Time	Off Going Nurse	On Coming Nurse

Date	Time	Off Going Nurse	On Coming Nurse
Date	Time	Off Going Nurse	On Coming Nurse

Date	Time	Off Going Nurse	On Coming Nurse
Date	Time	Off Going Nurse	On Coming Nurse

Date	Time	Off Going Nurse	On Coming Nurse
Date	Time	Off Going Nurse	On Coming Nurse

Date	Time	Off Going Nurse	On Coming Nurse
Date	Time	Off Going Nurse	On Coming Nurse

Date	Time	Off Going Nurse	On Coming Nurse
Date	Time	Off Going Nurse	On Coming Nurse

Date	Time	Off Going Nurse	On Coming Nurse

Date	Time	Off Going Nurse	On Coming Nurse

Date	Time	Off Going Nurse	On Coming Nurse
Date	Time	Off Going Nurse	On Coming Nurse

Date	Time	Off Going Nurse	On Coming Nurse
Date	Time	Off Going Nurse	On Coming Nurse

www.ingramcontent.com/pod-product-compliance
Lightning Source LLC
Chambersburg PA
CBHW081619250726
48657CB00009B/2628